W9-ATY-400

ACCESSORY
PROJECTS
FOR A
LAZY
CRAFTERNOON

BY STELLA FIELDS

CAPSTONE PRESS
a capstone imprint

Lazy Crafternoon and Savvy are published by
Capstone Press
A Capstone Imprint
1710 Roe Crest Drive
North Mankato, Minnesota 56003
www.mycapstone.com

Library of Congress Cataloging-in-Publication Data is available on the
Library of Congress website.

ISBN: 978-1-5157-1436-1

Summary: Use this craft book to spend a lazy crafternoon making
accessory projects with your friends.

Designer: Lori Bye
Creative Director: Heather Kindseth
Photos: Karon Dubke/Capstone Studio

Projects crafted by Lori Blackwell, Mari Bolte, Lori Bye,
Sarah Holden, Heather Kindseth, Marcy Morin, Sarah Schuette

Image credits: Shutterstock: Ann Haritonenko, back cover (bottom right), 5 (top right), 18, marilyn barbone,
13 (top), nenetus, 5 (top left), Pressmaster, 5 (bottom), wavebreakmedia, back cover (left)

Design Elements: Shutterstock: luanateutzi, Studio Lulu, Tossaporn Sakkabanchom

Special thanks to Dede Barton, Shelly Lyons, and Mari Bolte

Printed and bound in the USA.
009687F16

CONTENTS

LAZY CRAFTERNOON

A lazy crafternoon is a day you spend with your friends, each of you making something incredible. Doesn't sound lazy, right? But it can feel like it, especially with the fun, pretty accessory projects in this book.

These projects can be done on your own — nothing requires more than one person — but it's always more fun to spend a lazy crafternoon making things with your friends. The crafts in this book are great for beginners, but they can be taken to a new level by crafters with more experience. Invite girls who already craft on their own, but don't stop there. Your fashionista friend already has a great sense for fabric. Your musician friend knows how to put things together. Your movie-loving friend has an eye for what looks great.

You'll need plenty of supplies. You can choose projects from this book and stock the supplies yourself, or just ask your friends to bring what they have. Many of the projects here use things you already have around the house.

Before your friends arrive, get everything set up in your crafting space. You can craft on your bedroom floor or outside, but you might want to find a table where you can lay out the supplies and have room for everyone to work.

Snacks on sticks or cut into small, bite-sized pieces are great choices for people who don't want to get their hands dirty mid-craft. Check out page 28 for a perfect drink to serve your friends (and a craft to go along with it), and page 30 for a way to dress up a simple cake or cupcake.

That's it! Now get lazy.

SUPPLIES

beads
bottle cap
cardboard
cardstock
clear cell phone cover
colorful paper
craft knife
decoupage glue
earbud headphones
embroidery floss
eyeglass kit
fabric

needle and thread
paintbrush
pencil
pliers
polymer clay
ribbon
rubber bands
scissors
scrapbook paper

fabric paint
foam brush
freezer paper
glitter tape
hemp cord
hemp thread
iron
jump rings
leather cording
lollipop sticks
nail polish

shoes
skewers
star-shaped cookie cutter
stamp
straws
string
sunglasses
T-shirt
tagboard
toggle clasp
toothpick
washi tape
wire

Make a pretty phone case unlike anyone else's! You can personalize your phone in a snap.

WASHI PHONE CASE

WHAT YOU'LL NEED

clear cell phone cover
pencil
tagboard or cardstock
scissors
craft knife
washi and glitter tape

1. Trace the cell phone cover onto the tagboard. Be sure to include camera and microphone holes.

2. Cut out the tracing. Use the craft knife to cut out the camera and microphone holes.

3. Decorate the tagboard with tape. Try using various angles and lengths of tape. Washi and glitter tape can be layered, woven, cut, and adjusted as desired.

4. Place the tagboard tracing inside the cell phone cover, and insert the phone.

The great thing about this project is that you'll have plenty of supplies for multiple inserts. You can use a different one every day or swap them out whenever you want to. Make matching cases with your friends or use similar tape so your cases coordinate.

BRAIDED NECKLACE

Dress up a plain T-shirt with this perfect accessory.

2

3

5

6

WHAT YOU'LL NEED

fabric scraps
6 rubber bands
1-inch- (2.5-cm-) wide ribbon
needle and thread

1. Cut or tear your fabric into 1-inch- (2.5-cm-) wide lengths. Make three pieces about 18 inches (46 cm) long, three pieces that are 15 inches (38 cm) long, and three pieces that are 12 inches (30 cm) long.

2. Use a rubber band to put the three 18-inch- (46-cm-) long pieces together.

3. Braid the fabric pieces together. Use a rubber band to keep together at the end.

4. Repeat steps 1-3 twice with the other lengths.

5. Sew the end of each braid to keep it from unravelling.

6. Hold one end from each braid together and sew a 12-inch- (30-cm-) long piece of ribbon over the top of the braid. Do the same on the other side with the other end of the ribbon. Cut off any extra fabric.

To use your diffuser, apply a few drops of essential oil. Wait a few seconds for the oil to be absorbed before wearing your necklace.

DIFFUSER NECKLACES

A mood-uplifter you can wear (and it's so pretty, too)!

3

4

5

1 Knead the polymer clay with your hands until it's soft and pliable.

2 Pat or roll the clay out on your work surface until the clay is about 0.25 inch (0.6 cm) thick.

3 Use the bottle cap like a cookie cutter to cut out clay circles.

4 Decorate the clay circles with the stamp.

5 Make a hole near the top of each circle with the toothpick.

6 Set the clay circles on a baking sheet and bake according to the directions on the clay package. Let cool completely.

7 Cut a length of hemp thread about 24 inches (61 cm) long. Fold it in half and push the folded piece through the hole. Push the cut ends through the loop and pull the loop tight. Add one or two beads, knotting the thread after each bead, and knot the top to close.

Try some of these essential oils, alone or in combination:

HEADACHES: peppermint, frankincense, lavender
SLEEP: chamomile, lavender
ENERGY: peppermint, frankincense, lemon
RELAXATION: lavender, sandalwood, bergamot
MEMORY: rosemary, lemon
MOOD: lavender, lemon

All you need to make these adorable headbands is fabric, a needle, and thread.

FABRIC HEADBANDS TWO WAYS

TIED BOW HEADBAND

1   Measure and cut a piece of fabric about 6 inches (15 cm) wide by 22 inches (56 cm) long.

2   Fold the strip in half (with right sides together). Use a bottle cap to trace a half circle on both ends of the fabric.

3   Sew along one half circle and halfway down the long side of the fabric. Leave a 3-inch (7.5-cm) space and continue sewing down the long side of the fabric and the curve on the other end.

4   Trim off the extra fabric on the curves. Then flip right side out through the space in the seam.

5   Sew opening closed.

6   Wrap headband around head and tie with a double knot.

INFINITY HEADBAND

1   Cut two strips of fabric, each 6 inches wide (15 cm) and 22 inches (56 cm) long.

2   Fold each strip in half (with right sides together) and sew down the long side of raw edges, forming two tubes.

3   Flip the tubes right side out and lay them down, seam side up, in the shape of an X. Fold strips over so that they are linked together, matching up the raw edges.

4   Take unfinished headband and wrap around head, adjusting for proper fit. Then line up all raw edges and sew together. Cut off any excess.

Sewing tip: The right side of the fabric is the printed side. The other side is called the wrong side.

Pretty headphones that stand out in a crowd.

WRAPPED HEADPHONES

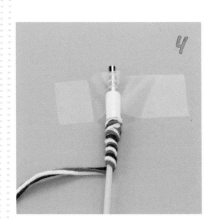

4

1 If using old earbuds, clean gently with soap and warm water.

2 Use the colored nail polish and toothpick to paint the earbuds and the headphone jack. Avoid painting anything metal or any parts that go in your ear. Also do not paint over any holes. When the nail polish is dry, use the clear topcoat to cover.

3 Cut the embroidery floss to about four times the length of the headphones cord.

4 Tie the floss to the plug end of the headphones. Hold down the ends and start wrapping.

5 Wrap until you reach the end of one earbud. To finish, just tie a knot and trim the edges. Then do the other earbud, starting the floss where the two sections separate.

You'll want to wear these sunglasses even when it's cloudy.

DECOUPAGE SUNGLASSES

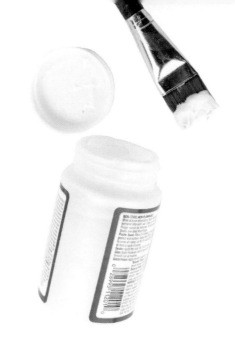

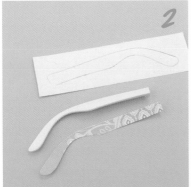

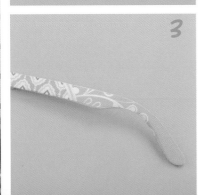

1 Use the screwdriver to remove the sunglasses' temples (the parts that go over your ears). Set the lenses and screws aside.

2 Trace the temples onto the scrapbook paper. Cut out and trim, if necessary.

3 Brush a thin layer of satin decoupage glue onto the outside of the temples. Stick the paper cutouts to them. Press out any creases or bubbles with your fingers. Let dry completely.

4 Place temples paper-side-up on a newspaper-lined work surface. Starting at one end, use a brush to cover the scrapbook paper with dimensional glue. Use a rag to catch any glue drips. Let dry completely. Repeat with the other sides of the temples.

5 Reattach the temples to the glasses' frame.

BEAD AND HEMP BRACELETS

Anyone would love these sweet bracelets for a fashionista.

WHAT YOU'LL NEED

leather cording
scissors
needle and thread
20 to 30 small beads
hemp cord
two jump rings
toggle clasp

1. Decide how long you would like your bracelet. Add 1 inch (2.5 cm), and then double the length. Cut the leather cording to that length.

2. Thread your needle with a 12-inch (30-cm) piece of thread. Tie a knot with the ends of the threads.

3. Thread all the beads onto the thread. Tie a knot at the end to secure, leaving a 1-inch (2.5-cm) tail. Cut off any excess thread.

4. Fold leather cording and tie the thread to the leather, creating a small leather loop.

5. Cut a 10-foot (3-meter) piece of hemp cord. Begin wrapping the hemp cord around the base of the leather loop. Be sure to tuck the hemp cord tail in while wrapping. Wrap the hemp cord until you reach the first bead.

6. Wrap the hemp cord between each bead once from left to right. When you get to the end of the bracelet, create a loop in the leather cord, and then wrap the hemp cord around the bracelet a few times.

7. Wrap the hemp cord back up the bracelet from right to left. When you reach your last bead, create another leather loop by tucking the end under the hemp wrapping. Cut off any excess hemp cord.

8. Attach a jump ring to each leather loop, and then attach toggle clasp to jump rings.

INFINITY SCARF

Stay cozy and warm in this gorgeous infinity scarf.

WHAT YOU'LL NEED

two pieces of fabric, each 14 inches
    (35.5 cm) wide and 72 inches
    (1.8 m) long
pins
scissors
needle and thread
buttons (optional)

1 Pin the right sides of the fabric pieces together. Then sew down each long side.

2 Flip right side out.

3 Sew the short ends together. Add buttons if you choose.

Try combining coordinating fabric!

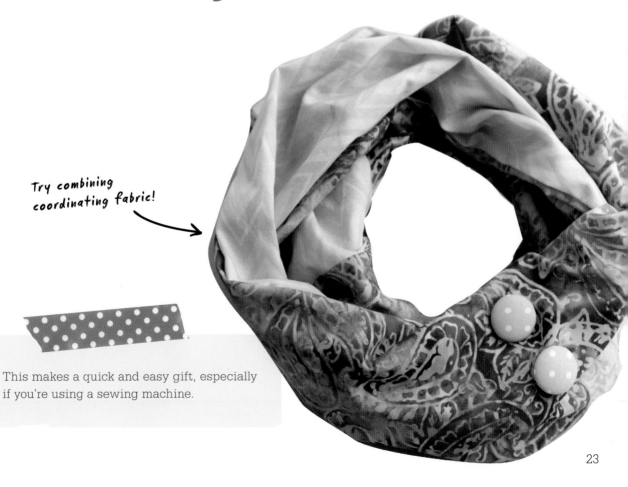

This makes a quick and easy gift, especially if you're using a sewing machine.

DECOUPAGE SHOES

Guarantee you'll have the most original shoes by decoupaging your own pair!

1. Cut out pieces of fabric or paper in whatever shapes you want.

2. Decide where you want to place the pieces on the shoes. They can be uneven or mismatched—whatever you think looks best.

3. Cover the first shoe with a layer of decoupage.

4. Carefully place each piece of fabric or paper on the shoe. Make sure that the piece is flat on the shoe and there are no air bubbles.

5. Repeat with the second shoe.

6. Cover both shoes in decoupage at least three times to seal your work. Let dry between each layer.

You can use an old comic book, magazine pages, heavyweight wrapping paper, scrapbooking paper, or fabric for this project. Your shoes will last longest if you keep them dry—no splashing in puddles!

GRAPHIC TEE

Plain T-shirts from the mall are so boring. Make your own!

WHAT YOU'LL NEED

pencil and paper
craft knife
freezer paper
T-shirt
iron
cardboard
fabric paint and paintbrush

1 Draw your design onto a piece of paper. When you're happy with it, set the freezer paper on top, shiny side down. Trace the design onto the freezer paper.

2 Put the freezer paper onto a protected work surface. (A big piece of cardboard or a clipboard works well for this part.) Use the craft knife to cut out the design.

3 Place a piece of cardboard inside the T-shirt. (This keeps your paint from bleeding through.) Using a low setting, iron the freezer paper stencil onto the T-shirt. The stencil should feel secure and not move.

4 Paint over the stencil using the fabric paint. You may need several coats. Let the paint dry completely between coats.

5 When the paint is dry, use a low setting to iron the front of the shirt. Then peel off the stencil. When you wash your shirt, make sure to turn it inside out.

When cutting your stencil, keep in mind that the parts you're cutting out are the parts that will get painted. You'll either need to make sure it's all one piece, or keep track of any small pieces

You can reuse your pattern to make another shirt with the same print, but for best results, cut a new stencil for each shirt.

SUNRISE SIPPER AND STAR CHARMS

This glittery mocktail is made even sweeter with a coordinating drink charm.

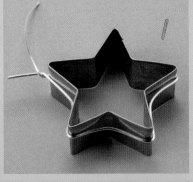

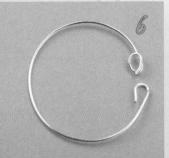

SUNRISE SIPPERS

1 Mix the sugar and edible glitter together on a small, shallow plate. Run the orange wedge around the edge of the glass, then turn the glass upside down to dip the lip in the sugar.

2 Flip the glass right side up. Pour a little grenadine into the bottom of the glass. Fill the glass two-thirds full with orange juice. Then add pineapple juice until the glass is full. Put the orange wedge on the edge of the glass as shown.

STAR CHARMS

1 Wrap a length of 20g wire around the contours of a small star-shaped cookie cutter. Use a small pliers to twist the two ends together.

2 Make a small loop with one end of the wire. Twist the wire below the loop twice, leaving a small tail of wire.

3 Twist the other end around the bottom of the loop. Cut off the extra wire.

4 Remove the wire star from the cookie cutter.

5 Cut a long length of thin-gauge wire. Twist one end of the wire to the star shape. Slide assorted beads onto the wire. Wrap the wire and beads around the star shape until you like how it looks. Then twist the end of the wire around itself and cut off the excess. Set the star charm aside.

6 Cut a 2-inch (5-cm) length of wire. Wrap it around a small, round object (like a spool of thread). Make sure that the ends of the wire overlap about 0.5 inch (1.2 cm). Using a small pliers, turn one end of the wire into a loop, and bend the other end into a hook. Connect the two.

7 Slide the star charm onto the charm loop.

Even the sweetest of cakes can be made sweeter with this little banner.

CAKE BANNER

1. Cut cardstock into ½-inch by 3-inch (1.2-cm by 7.5-cm) strips.

2. Place string on your workspace. Place the cardstock strips on the string so that the short end of each strip rests against the string.

3. One strip at a time, fold washi tape over the string and cardstock.

4. Trim the tape and cardstock into flag shapes and discard any excess tape and cardstock.

5. String your DIY washi bunting between two lollipop sticks or straws and stick onto the top of your cake or cupcake.

2

3

READ MORE

Bolte, Mari. *Eco Gifts: Upcycled Gifts You Can Make.* Make It, Gift It. North Mankato, Minn.: Capstone Press, 2016.

Low, Rachel. *Girl's Guide to DIY Fashion: Design & Sew 5 Complete Outfits.* Lafayette, Calif.: C&T Publishing, 2015.

Friedrichsen-Truman, Christina. *Rubber Band Glam: A Rainbow of Dazzling Beaded Designs for Bracelets, Accessories, and More.* Beverly, Mass.: Quarry Books, 2015.

INTERNET SITES

FactHound offers a safe, fun way to find Internet sites related to this book. All of the sites on FactHound have been researched by our staff.

Here's all you do:
Visit www.facthound.com
Type in this code: 9781515714361

LOOK FOR ALL THE BOOKS IN THE SERIES